Guess Where You're Going, Guess What You'll Do

A. F. Bauman

Illustrated by True Kelley

Houghton Mifflin Company

Boston

For my mother,
Mildred J. Welch — A. F. B.

For Nicky Dilmore — T. K.

Library of Congress Cataloging-in-Publication Data

Bauman, A. F. (Anne F.)
  Guess where you're going, guess what you'll do / A.F. Bauman;
illustrated by True Kelley.
    p.   cm.
    Summary: After a variety of situations are described, the reader
is invited to guess resulting destinations and activities which are
then revealed on a subsequent page.
    ISBN 0-395-50211-X
    [1. Picture puzzles.]   I. Kelley, True, ill.   II. Title.
III. Title: Guess where you are going, guess what you will do.
PZ7.B3274Gu   1989   89-30065
[E]—dc19   CIP
                             AC

Printed in the United States of America

WOZ   10   9   8   7   6   5   4   3   2

Birthday parties, tea parties,
taking walks, and flying kites.
There are so many things to do,
so many places to go.
As you read this book,
can you guess where you're going?
Can you guess what you'll do?

You wake to a wonderful surprise:
a world that's white and sparkling.
Put on your warmest clothes
and a pair of boots.
Find your mittens and a hat.
Stuff some tissues in your pocket,
and get ready to sail over mounds
of soft snow.

Guess where you're going.
Guess what you'll do.

5

Spring is here!
Take a ball to toss or a
Frisbee to throw outdoors.
Some icy lemonade will
quench your thirst.
Hungry? Pack yourself a
thick sandwich of cold ham
and cheese.

Guess where you're going.
Guess what you'll do.

TRASH

Help Keep Our
City Beautiful

Pull on a sweatshirt and
an old pair of jeans.
Rubber boots will keep
your feet dry.
Fill a can with
dirt and fat worms.
Take along some strong line
and lots of time.

Guess where you're going.
Guess what you'll do.

13

The sun is hot
and so are you.
Fill your tote bag
with summer things:
a tube of sunscreen,
a big fluffy towel,
and a comb to get
the tangles
out of your wet hair.
Now you're ready
to beat the heat.

Guess where you're going.
Guess what you'll do.

The sun is rising and
Mom's getting breakfast.
Time to get up
and get dressed.
Put pencils and crayons
into your backpack.
Leave room for a
peanut butter sandwich,
potato chips, and an apple.
Don't be late!

Guess where you're going.
Guess what you'll do.

A big yellow moon
hangs in the sky.
Dress up in crazy clothes.
Take a flashlight
and a paper bag.
You'll have more fun
if you go with your friends.
It's the scariest, spookiest
night of the year!

Guess where you're going.
Guess what you'll do.

Put on pajamas and
turn on the night-light.
Settle down with your teddy bear
and listen to a good story
while the moon comes up.
It's been a long, long day.

Guess where you're going.
Guess what you'll do.

Where will you go,
what will you do tomorrow?